Dedication

I wrote Martina from my desire to not see children suffer from the terror of abuse. It's my hope that we will speak out to protect our children from such horrors and help them to have safe, happy childhoods.

I ask God to bless the life of each of those who come to have this copy in their hands, that their eternal purpose be fulfilled in their lives and we can be of help to many.

I dedicate this book to my beloved nephews Alejo, Chris, Nico, Cami, Nico M, Ethan and my nieces Abby, Juli and Jill. You have made my heart overflow with pure love. To Karen, Kaelen, Keira, Jamie, Callum, Zoe, Samuel, Arabelle and Andres you hold a special place in my heart, too. Mateo, Guera Pao and Isaac you are my little warriors of faith. For my future children as well, you all inspire me to want a better world for you.

To my husband Edison Cespedes, my parents and brother who are my greatest motivators. I cannot forget the rest of my family, sponsors and friends; especially Tatiana, Cynthia and Lupita. None of this would be possible without you.

To Bibiana Puente P, my friend and illustrator who, like a second self, captured my heart in each drawing. Thanks to my friend Karol Paz for believing in me, for encouraging me to dream and persevere in this project, through her company Ixoye, her family and friendship bless my life.

To my uncle-grandfather, Jairo Buitrago, for sharing his love of writing. I thank God for the lives of my friends and project partners Johana Nikepha and Karina Bolivar, without your prayers, support and talents this would not be a reality.

To my pastors and friends, Claudia and Diego Rodríguez for your inspiration and support. Last, but certainly not least, I thank my Lord, Jesus Christ for being the beginning and the end of this. I give You all the honor and glory.

Luisa F. Segura

God has given each of us artistic gifts that we often take for granted. I thank my Heavenly Father for allowing me to take the gift I first discovered at 11 years-old and use it to bring this story to life.

I am grateful for my husband, Johnathan Paz, who encouraged me to believe in my own ability and for Luisa Segura for trusting me with her story and allowing me to illustrate her ideas.

I also thank my sister-in-law, Karol Paz, for insisting that I think BIG, assuring me that with God all things are possible. To my uncle, Mauricio Acevedo, who guided me step-by-step with this project and his graphic design skills. His artwork is a timeline of my life. I am grateful for my siblings who share in this artistic gift as well.

To my nephew and other children that I have worked with, I hope that these illustrations will help you protect yourself against abuse.

I want to thank my parents because they are always proud of my achievements.

Bibiana Puente P.

I believe that this book was a great and inspirational story. It teaches kids that they don't need to fear to tell others how they feel and if they ever need help that they can tell a trusted adult. I think this book is a great lesson for kids to learn about trusting God with their emotions and that they should be able to learn from their mistakes and move on from their past feelings. And if any kids feel fear or discomfort that they are never alone. God will always be by their side. I believe kids will learn that even if someone does something that hurts them physically or mentally that they should always forgive them for what they did, and that God also forgives them.

- Ammy Zea Paz.
13 years old.

I think that this is a child friendly way to show smaller children about a problem in this world and how not to be scared about coming out and telling people about what they're going through and that if they feel uncomfortable with someone they should tell an adult or someone they trust.

- Eddie Emmanuel Rodriguez P.
13 years old.

I think that this is an interesting book to read and it can show kids to not keep secrets from their parents and it can show them that your parents will always help you when you are sad and it is ok to tell your parents what you are feeling or if someone or something is bothering you.

- Camila
11 years old.

I think that this book is inspiring and interesting because it shows to not be scared to tell your parents anything that you feel uncomfortable about and that your parents will always support you no matter what.

- Hannah Zea Paz
12 years old.

The sun shined gloriously as it peeked through the curtains. What a beautiful morning to celebrate!

"Happy birthday my girl!", Leticia said, kissing her daughter on the forehead.

"Happy birthday beautiful princess!", her father Juan said beaming at her proudly.

"Happy birthday Tina!", the twins shouted in unison. Carlos and Ana came running with two enormous balloons. "It's your big day, Tina!", Ana yelled with excitement.

"I know Ana, today is the day. Isn't it Mommy?"

"Yes sweetheart, but why are you so excited?"

"Mommy, I have been waiting for three long years to get this. It's going to be the best present of my life!"

"I know, I know dear. You've been eager for this one. Come on, we'll wait for you in the kitchen."

"I'm coming…"

DEAR DIARY:

 I am so glad that I can write in you today. I thought this day

 would never come! I will write about my adventures, but for

 now, I have a gift to open. Don't worry, I will always let you be

 part of my story.

Martina

My Favorite birthday memory

Finally! There it is! Somewhere between all the balloons and everyone's curiosity was a beautiful gold box with a giant red ribbon. The slightly faded card read,

"For my little Martina"
WITH ALL MY LOVE. MAMMA JUANITA.

It was the treasure box that my grandma left for me before she went to heaven. It was precious because it held so many special memories. My Grandma gave it to my Mom for me before she died for safekeeping.

She got it from her father, and I would get it on my eighth birthday.

He was my great-grandfather, and he brought it home after the war. It's filled with his special letters.

Grandma gave it to Mom when she was eight and told her to fill it with sweet memories. After Mom married, she gave it back to grandma to keep it safe for me. They collected many beautiful stones that were hidden in different places in the garden. Now I must find them.

Today is the day I get it! This is the note that was inside.

Dear Martina,

I am so proud of you. I thank God that I am leaving this treasure box in the hands of my charming, special girl. You are always so happy, kind, and full of love. Every stone has a powerful word and each one tells a story. Your mother and I collected them. I hope they will be as valuable to you as they have been to us and will be a precious memory forever. Guard this treasure box but most of all.
"Keep your heart with all vigilance, for from it flow the springs of life"
PROVERBS 4:23

WITH LOVE, MAMMA JUANITA.

"Mom, why did my grandma ask me to do this? Why did she want me to collect the stones and honor each word?"

"They are to teach you. Just as they taught me and your Uncle Cesar. She wanted to be sure that I would teach my children too. I know that she is overjoyed today as I have four treasures — Daddy, Ana, Carlos and you."

"You forgot Kitty Mommy", Martina said, frowning.

"Of course! Kitty too", Leticia chuckled to herself.

"Kitty and my diary were the first gifts Mamma Juanita left me. But today I'm starting a new adventure with my treasure box", Martina said proudly.

"Yes sweetie."

"I love you Mom!"

"And I love you darling."

"Tina, Tina, Tina! Where are you?" Carlos said with a mischievous grin.
"In here Carlos. What happened?" Martina was startled by his sudden presence.
"We made something for you!", Carlos said, reaching towards her.
"Wow…. what a beautiful plaque, thank you!"
"And I made the flower.", said Ana.
"Thanks. It's beautiful!" Tina said, admiring the small metal plaque. Dad helped the twins paint it. It was beautiful.
"Martina bring your box, we'll put the plaque in there," Dad said with an enormous smile.

"Great! Let's have fun in the garden! It's such a nice day."
Leticia looked for a shady place to put her wooden chair. It was her favorite place to sit and watch the children's adventures in the garden. She smiled, watching them search for the hidden treasures.

"Come on twins. Let's go! Let's find some stones for my treasure box!" Martina was so excited she could hardly wait for them to catch up.
"I'll wash them and clean them for you!", Ana was delighted while Carlos was digging through his toy box looking for shovels and rakes.
"Don't ruin my flowers.", Leticia warned.
"We won't! We won't!", the children sang in unison.

It was a festive day. The children were brimming with laughter as they searched for stones. The children had done a good job searching for the stones. They found a beautiful turquoise stone with the word LOVE written on it.

"This word represents our family. This is us!", Martina told them.

Tina gently touched the stone to her face. "Tina, What are you thinking of?", Carlos quizzed.
"Mamma Juanita.", she said thoughtfully.

"Tina, do you remember her?", Ana asked.

Martina smiled and let out a deep sigh. "Yes, she was sweet and beautiful. I know we were young, but I remember her love for us and how proud she was."

They went inside to search for pictures of her, from the twins second birthday. It was just a few weeks after that she passed away.

"That was our last photo with her." Tina gently sat the picture on the coffee table with a thoughtful smile.

Searching for the stones turned into an exhausting day. Filled with excitement one moment and disappointment the next. It was hard to find the stones to fill the treasure box.

As they searched, the twins became curious as to the meaning of words written on the stones and just what they meant to grandma.

DEAR DIARY:

I know that I don't use you as much as I used to, but I must tell you about the 15 stones found during these three adventurous months. The turquoise stone had love written on it. The pink one had respect. Then an esmerald green stone had happiness, and the yellow had patience. There were other stones, too. Red, white, black and gray which had friendship, peace, tolerance and sweetness. There was a purple stone that said honesty and a silver one with pleasure. Then the orange one said faith, and the lilac was gentleness. There was a gold one for kindness and sky blue for self-control. Most beautiful of all was the rainbow stone written with forgiveness. Mom says that we must treasure them in our heart and use them in our dealings with others. I feel thrilled and fortunate. Sometimes it seems easy, at other times not. Oh! I forgot! My 16-year-old cousin is coming to visit us, and it is about three years since we have seen him. Dad says he is a very special and talented young man. I look forward to showing him my Treasure Box.

Tina set up a small table and chair for a tea party with her favorite porcelain doll. Chattering with excitement, she said, "It's a beautiful Saturday! That means family breakfast, fun and games with the twins and starting my ballet lessons again.

Today I also get to see my big cousin, Mike. He's my father's nephew. He is the best basketball player on his school team! At least that's what his Dad, Uncle Raul, says. I think he'll give us some lessons." Tina was so excited she couldn't wait.

"Mike is here! Mike is here", the children screamed. He always had time for us. He had so much patience with Carlos. He showed Carlos so many basketball tricks. Carlos wasn't the best at basketball, but Mike made him feel good.

He told Carlos with two weeks of practice with him, he'd be like a pro. Mike was our hero. He didn't mind that the girls hung around, either. Most adults get tired of kids, but Mike always had time for us.

Mike was loving and charming and seemed to be having the time of his life. This was turning out to be the best summer vacation.

Every day he wanted to know more and more about the treasure box and just what was in it. Martina was thrilled by his interest.

With all the games, fun and laughter, this was turning out to be a great visit.

After a long hot day of running, laughing and playing everyone was exhausted. Mike slept in the room next to Martina's. A summer storm kicked up that night and Mike came running into her room and sat on her bed and began touching her hair.

Martina woke from her sleep. "What are you doing here?", she muttered. "I only came to see if you were alright." He said still stroking her hair. Martina was uncomfortable but didn't know what to say. "The thunder is loud, she managed.

"That's why I came Martina. Can I stay awhile?"
Martina hesitated, unsure what to do, but she nodded her head.

Martina felt like there was a hole in her stomach, her heart began to beat quickly. Mike began to stroke her hair in a way that made her feel sick. She felt a terror she had never felt before.

Pulling away, she asked, "What are youuuu doing?"

I just want to show you, you're my favorite cousin. Don't worry, this is our secret. He kissed her hand and left her room.

Martina was confused. She didn't know exactly what it was, but something made her feel uncomfortable. The next day she was not herself at all. Her usual happy smile simply faded away.

Everywhere she turned, it seemed that Mike was close by. Twice he whispered in her ear. "Don't forget our secret. It's as special as your treasure chest."

Martina went to sleep that night deep in thought. Her treasure box made her very happy, but she was also very sad. She was confused. What really happened that night with Mike?

He came to her room again, touching her hair. He filled her with fear and doubt. She felt angry and hurt and didn't know what to do. He even tried to touch her private parts. She jumped off the bed so fast. "Leave right now! I said leave or I'll scream". She was so frightened she began to tremble.

"Calm down! You know I care about you. You are so special to me. I want to make something special for us... but, it must be our secret.", Mike said. "Rest now and tomorrow we'll share a special surprise before I leave." Mike left the room.

The next day at breakfast...

"Tina, pass me the milk please. Tina, Tina! Are you listening?", Carlos asked. What is wrong with you? What's happening to you?
"Oh, it's nothing. Sorry. I was just thinking," Tina said, barely lifting her head.
"OK, slow pokes, we have to take Mike to the airport. Get ready. There isn't much time." Mom said as she walked out of the dining room.
"We're going to miss you, Mike!" The twins were running, jumping and hugging him.

One by one everyone hugged Mike to say goodbye. Mom, Dad and the twins seemed sad to see him go. As he hugged Martina, he gave her a small bag. He whispered, "I hope you had fun. Remember, what happened between us is our special secret".

Tina pulled away. She shrugged her shoulders and dropped her head.

When Martina got home, she opened the bag. It was her treasure box. It was empty!

There were no stones in it, only a note...

"Tina I only took your stones to bring more emotion to your treasure box, they are hidden throughout the house, I hope you enjoy looking for them again. Keep our secret in the treasure box." With love, your cousin Mike.

Tina began to cry. She was inconsolable. She was filled with rage. "Where are my stones?", she yelled. Everything was in chaos.
"Tina, Tina, Are you crying? You miss Mike?", Ana asked sweetly.
"No! I never want to see him again! Leave me alone! Leave me alone!"
Ana was confused. She had never seen Tina act this way. "Want to play?" She didn't know what else to say.
Ana was worried. She searched for her Mom. "Mommy, mommy." She ran to her. Something is wrong with Tina. She is angry, and she's crying. It's like she's not even my sister anymore."
"Don't say that!", Leticia scolded. "I'll go talk to her. You go outside with Daddy and Carlos. I will find her."
Leticia found Tina in her room crying hysterically. She was angry. "Where are my stones? Everything is so mixed-up?", Tina shouted.

Leticia had never seen such an attitude from Martina. "What's wrong, my love?" She tried her best to comfort her. "Leave me alone", Tina sobbed.

"What has happened? I'm your Mom. You can tell me anything. I love you." Tina fell in her mother's arms sobbing and holding her tightly. She shoved Leticia the note from cousin Mike and her empty treasure box. Leticia tightened her lips and shook her head. "Don't cry. We will find them again." Then her eyes fell on the words "our secret" and her heart quickened.

"What secret do you have with Mike?", Leticia asked.

"I… I… I… I don't know if I should tell you," Tina said as she backed away. Leticia was getting worried. "Why not? Why wouldn't you tell your mother?"

"Because you can't tell secrets, Mom. You said so. Remember?"

"Tina, there are good secrets and bad secrets." She hugged Tina tight.

"How do you know which is which?", asked Tina.

"A bad secret will make you sad, angry or ashamed of yourself.", Leticia said as she sat in the very rocking chair that she rocked Tina in as a baby.
"A good secret makes you happy and inspires you. You never have to keep a good secret forever. Remember the present we made for Dad for Father's Day? That secret made us so happy." She said as she giggled. We couldn't wait to tell him and show him.
Martina listened attentively.
"Now, tell me, what kind of secret are you keeping? Good?"
Martina didn't need to think about it. She hurried to her Mom and hugged her so tight. Slowly she began to tell her what happened with Mike the last two night while everyone was sleeping.
They cried and hugged. Martina felt her Mom's love and support.
"Did I let grandma down?", Leticia sniffled as she asked.
"Why would you say that? It's not your fault, Tina. It's not your fault."
"I didn't guard my treasure box. He took all my stones! All my treasure is gone. I didn't even notice it was missing.", Tina was so sorry,

"Don't say that, sweetheart. Take it easy. Now wash your face and I'll go make us tea. Let's talk a bit." Leticia took her time as she prepared the tea. If was difficult to see Martina like this.

Leticia returned to the bedroom. "When I was looking for a spoon for the sugar, I found two of your stones—forgiveness and love. Maybe that's a good place to start.

"Please forgive me for not realizing what Mike was doing. I'm so sorry. You must forgive yourself, too. This was not your fault. I know it's hard dear, but we must also learn to forgive Mike, even though he must face consequences for his actions."

"Most of all, you must believe that your heart is God's treasure. Every good thing he has given you like love and joy and peace can never be taken away."

"You know what?", said Leticia lovingly. "The treasure box is like your heart. It will never be empty. It will always be filled with love. Just like you, all children deserve to be happy.

They deserve to feel safe about their bodies, their feelings and their surroundings. Adults are to protect children as they learn and grow to love themselves. "I am so proud of you Tina. You have so much courage. I'm glad you told me this."

It was hard to do, but Juan and Leticia spoke to Mike's parents. They wanted to know why Mike did this.

They also wanted Mike's parents to send him to a counselor and speak with their pastor to keep this from happening again. In the meantime, they would focus their attention on Tina and trust Jesus to heal their hearts.

It took some time, but Martina found her stones and with them her happiness. Through this entire ordeal Martina learn to share her heart with God and strengthen her relationship with her family. She even taught the twins the differences between a good secret and a bad one.

Juan and Leticia also found community support for Tina. Where she could share her feelings and help other children who had experienced this kind of behavior.

To grow-up healthy and happy is our right. Our hearts are a treasure we must care for. When we fill it with the most precious stones to help us in difficult moments, it will bring us happiness in life's beautiful moments.

Copyright © 2021 Luisa Segura.
All rights reserved.

No part of this publication may be reproduced, distributed, or transmitted in any form or by any means, including photocopying, recording, or other electronic or mechanical methods, without the prior written permission of the publisher, except in the case of brief quotations embodied in critical reviews and certain other noncommercial uses permitted by copyright law.

For permission requests, write to the publisher, addressed "Attention: Permissions Coordinator," at the address below. Any references to historical events, real people, or real places are used fictitiously. Names, characters, and places are products of the author's imagination.

ISBN: 978-1-7359997-3-9 (Paperback)
Library of Congress Control Number: 002241827
Illustrator by Artist Bibiana Puente.
Book design by Designer Alejandra Carreon.
Printed in United States of America. First printed edition 2021.
www.FundacionCaminaConmigo.com

www.ingramcontent.com/pod-product-compliance
Lightning Source LLC
Chambersburg PA
CBHW061401090426
42743CB00002B/96